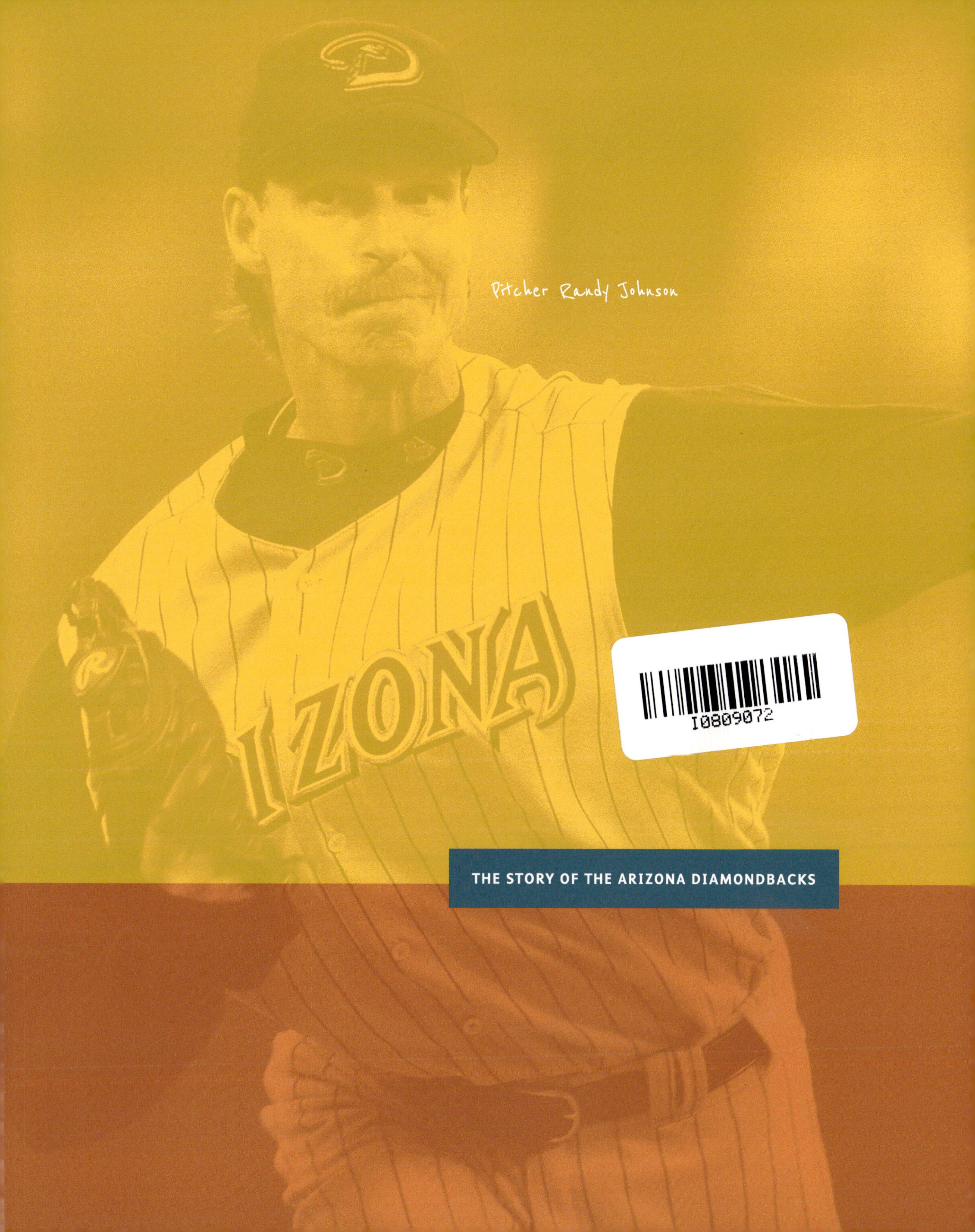

Pitcher Randy Johnson

THE STORY OF THE ARIZONA DIAMONDBACKS

Third baseman Eugenio Suárez

THE STORY OF THE

ARIZONA DIAMONDBACKS

JIM WHITING

CREATIVE SPORTS

First baseman Christian Walker

CREATIVE EDUCATION / CREATIVE PAPERBACKS

Published by Creative Education and Creative Paperbacks
P.O. Box 227, Mankato, Minnesota 56002
Creative Education and Creative Paperbacks are imprints of
The Creative Company
www.thecreativecompany.us

Book Design by Wyeth Morgan
Art direction by Blue Design (www.bluedes.com)

Images by Alamy Stock Photo/Cal Sport Media, 7 (bottom, left), Chris Brown, 20, Kevin Dietsch, 16; Associated Press/Brynn Anderson, 29, 31, Frank Jansky/Icon Sportswire, cover, Jeff Roberson, 7 (top, left), Ross D. Franklin, 2; Getty Images/Al Bello, 12, Brian Bahr, 4–5, 7 (top, right), Christian Petersen, 18, 32, Dilip Vishwanat, 25, Don Smith, 6 (bottom, left), Dustin Bradford, 3, Harry How, 11, Jed Jacobsohn, 1, 7 (bottom, right), Jeff Carlick, 6 (bottom, right), Jeff Gross, cover, 9, 10, Jonathan Daniel, 15, Kansas City Star, 24, Nick Cammett/Diamond Images, 30, Paul Spinelli, 22–23, RHONA WISE, 26–27, Rob Leiter, 10, Stephen Dunn, 6 (top, right), 19; Wikimedia Commons/All–Pro Reels, 6 (top, left)

Library of Congress Cataloging-in-Publication Data
Names: Whiting, Jim, 1943- author
Title: The story of the Arizona Diamondbacks / by: Jim Whiting.
Other titles: Arizona Diamondbacks
Description: [New edition.] | Mankato, Minnesota : Creative Education and Creative Paperbacks, [2026] | Series: Creative sports : Major League baseball | Includes index. | Audience: Ages 8-12 | Audience: Grades 4-6 | Summary: "Discover the Arizona Diamondbacks' thrilling journey as they rose from an expansion team to World Series champions, featuring legendary players, pivotal moments, and the Major League Baseball team's enduring resilience and determination. Written for middle-grade readers. Includes table of contents, sidebars, and index"– Provided by publisher.
Identifiers: LCCN 2025013161 (print) | LCCN 2025013162 (ebook) | ISBN 9798895810842 library binding | ISBN 9798896800378 paperback | ISBN 9798895812105 ebook
Subjects: LCSH: Arizona Diamondbacks (Baseball team)–History–Juvenile literature
Classification: LCC GV875. A64 W55 2026 (print) | LCC GV875.A64 (ebook) | DDC 796.357640979173–dc23/eng/20250512
LC record available at https://lccn.loc.gov/2025013161
LC ebook record available at https://lccn.loc. gov/2025013162

Printed in the United States

Pitcher Mike Myers

TUCKER
20

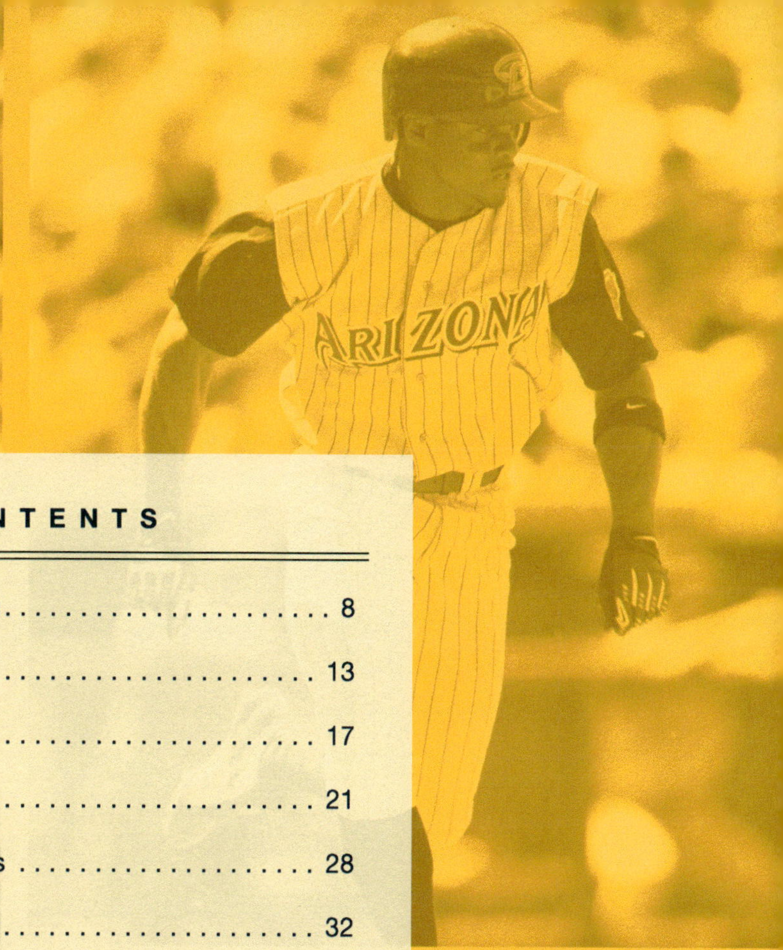

CONTENTS

The Long and Short of It 8

A Hot Start 13

Worst to First 17

Reshaping the Roster 21

Back to the World Series 28

Index 32

EXTRA INNINGS

Gonzo 10

A Perfect Night 15

Hidden Gem 16

The Most Valuable 20

Law of Averages 27

The Long Wait Is Over 29

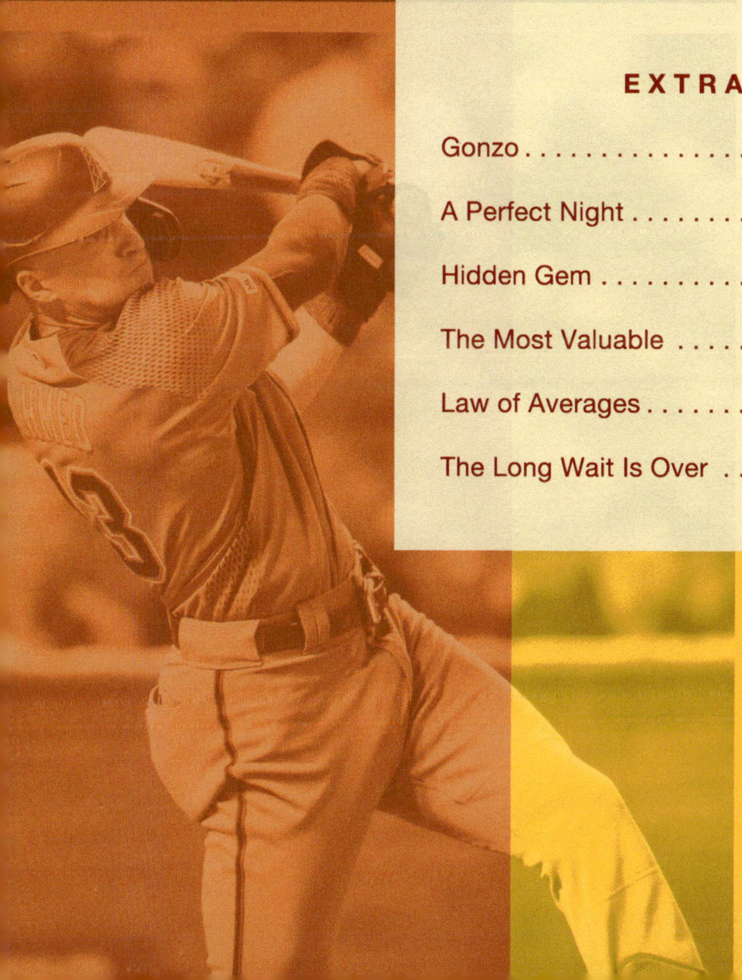

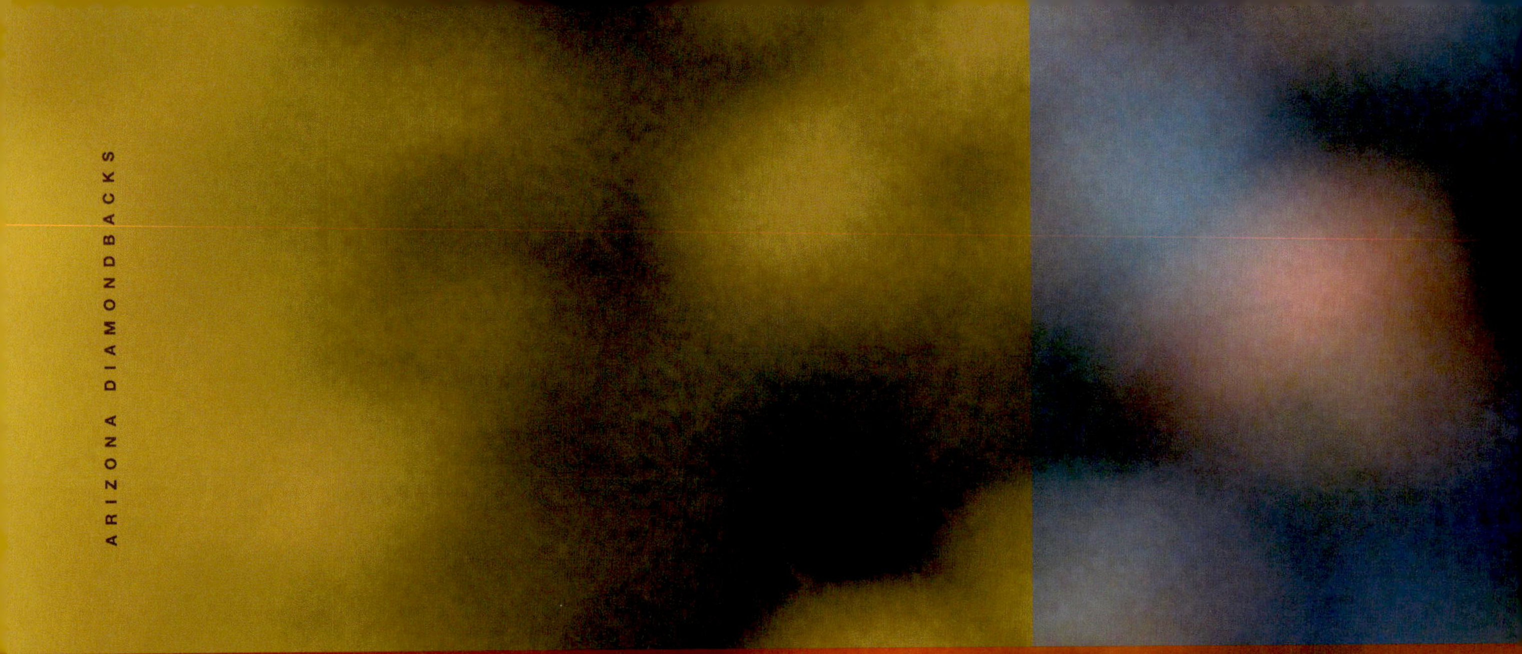

THE LONG AND SHORT OF IT

Game 7 of the 2001 World Series featured a classic batter-pitcher matchup in the bottom of the ninth inning. Arizona Diamondbacks outfielder Luis Gonzalez stepped into the batter's box. He hit 57 homers and drove in 142 runs during the regular season. He faced Mariano Rivera of the New York Yankees. Rivera was generally regarded as the top reliever in Major League Baseball (MLB)—not just that season but of all time. Rivera's best pitch was the cut fastball. It was especially effective against left-handed batters. It broke toward their hands at the last moment. It was almost impossible to get the barrel of the bat onto the ball. And Gonzalez batted left.

Tonight Rivera had struck out the side in the eighth inning to preserve New York's 2–1 lead. He wasn't as effective in the ninth. With one out and runners on first and second, he gave up a double to light-hitting shortstop Tony Womack. That tied the score at 2–2. Rivera hit the next batter to load the bases. That brought up "Gonzo," as he was nicknamed.

No one could have foreseen this situation just four years earlier. The Diamondbacks opened National League (NL) play in 1998 as an expansion team. The team name recognized

Outfielder Luis Gonzalez

EXTRA INNINGS

LUIS GONZALEZ
LEFT FIELD
DIAMONDBACKS SEASONS: 1999–2006
HEIGHT: 6-FOOT-2
WEIGHT: 180 POUNDS
KEY STATS: .298 BATTING AVERAGE, 224 HOME RUNS, 774 RBIS, 3X ALL-STAR

GONZO

Luis Gonzalez broke into the big leagues in 1990 with the Houston Astros. He played for two other teams before landing in Arizona. It was one of the best deals in team history. When he arrived, he had a reputation as a solid contact hitter. He was better known for line drives than home runs. But in Arizona, the slim outfielder turned into a home-run-hitting slugger. He knocked 224 balls out of the park as a Diamondbacks player. He was named to three All-Star teams. In 2010, he became the first member of the Diamondbacks to have his jersey number (20) retired.

From left, pitcher Curt Schilling and owner Jerry Colangelo

the region's native rattlesnakes. The D-backs lost their first five games. That set the tone for the rest of the season. Arizona won just 65 games. Only the Florida Marlins had a worse record in the league.

It was a very different story four years later. Arizona faced the Yankees in the World Series. New York was the defending champion. They were heavily favored. It all came down to the deciding Game 7 and the duel between Gonzalez and Rivera.

Fans who packed Bank One Ballpark in Phoenix, Arizona, were on their feet. Many hoped that Gonzo would smash the ball into the seats.

He fouled off the first pitch. Then Rivera jammed him with his cut fastball. "I knew the infield was playing in [and] didn't have to try and hit it hard, just loop something out there and get it in play," Gonzalez said.

That was exactly what he did. Yankee shortstop Derek Jeter could only watch helplessly as the ball flew over his head and landed a few feet beyond the infield onto the outfield grass. Arizona second baseman Jay Bell romped home with the winning run. It was one of the shortest base hits of Gonzo's career, but it made for the most iconic moment in Diamondbacks history. Arizona had won its first World Series crown!

ARIZONA

A HOT START

The 2001 World Series crown was a tribute to Diamondbacks owner Jerry Colangelo's determination to be immediately competitive. Even before the team played its first game in 1998, he signed players such as shortstop/second baseman Jay Bell, third baseman Matt Williams, and pitcher Andy Benes to big contracts.

Colangelo was just getting started. In 1999, he inked deals with top-notch players such as Gold Glove-winning center fielder Steve Finley, speedy shortstop Tony Womack, and Gonzalez. Gonzo impressed his new fans with a breakout season. He finished with a .336 batting average, a league-leading 206 hits, 111 runs batted in (RBIs), and 26 home runs. He also had a 30-game hitting streak.

Perhaps the most important signing Colangelo snagged was left-handed pitcher Randy Johnson. With his wild hair, shaggy moustache, and towering 6-foot-10 height, Johnson was an intimidating presence. Nicknamed the "Big Unit," his nearly 100-mile-per hour fastball and tricky slider terrorized opposing batters. He won the first of his four consecutive Cy Young Awards that season.

The moves paid off. Arizona won a whopping 100 games in 1999. Just one NL team had more wins. The 35-win differential from one season to another is the best in MLB history.

Not only that, but Arizona also became the first expansion team to advance to the playoffs in just its second season. But the New York Mets defeated the D-backs in the National League Division Series (NLDS), three games to one.

Injuries slowed the team in 2000. Star pitcher Curt Schilling arrived in July via a trade with the Philadelphia Phillies. But that was not enough to boost the Diamondbacks. Arizona compiled an 85–77 mark. It missed the playoffs.

Third baseman Matt Williams

Johnson and Schilling combined for 43 wins in 2001. They finished first and second in almost every MLB pitching statistic as Arizona won the NL West. It charged into the NLDS against the St. Louis Cardinals. The teams split the first four games. Then the Diamondbacks edged the Redbirds 2–1 in Game 5. Arizona advanced to the National League Championship Series (NLCS) against the Atlanta Braves. The Diamondbacks won easily, taking four of five games.

That sent Arizona to the World Series. The home team won each of the first six games. It looked like this pattern might be broken in Game 7 as Arizona's bats went quiet. The Yankees led 2–1 going into the bottom of the ninth before Gonzalez's bloop single won the series.

"From day one, our goal wasn't just to get to the World Series," Gonzalez said. "It was to win it." Three days later, a parade drew more than 300,000 exuberant fans.

Arizona's fans hoped for the same success the following season. They got it—sort of. Despite a rash of injured players, the fine pitching of Johnson and Schilling helped the team win 98 games. Arizona secured the division crown again. But the Cardinals swept the NLDS in three games.

The injury bug returned in 2003. It bit Johnson, Schilling, and several other key players. Suddenly, the formerly veteran-heavy team was populated with youngsters called up from the minor leagues. Thirteen rookies, called the "Baby Backs," debuted during the season. One was pitcher Brandon Webb. He won 10 games and posted a 2.84 earned run average (ERA). The season ended respectably at 84–78. But it wasn't good enough for the playoffs.

Arizona set about revamping the roster before the 2004 season. "It's going to be exciting," Arizona general manager Joe Garagiola Jr. said of the new acquisitions. "This will give our whole lineup a very different look." Unfortunately, more injuries and subpar performances led to a dismal 51–111 mark. It was one of the worst records in MLB's modern era. One of the few highlights came when Johnson pitched a perfect game. Despite that, the team traded him after the season.

EXTRA INNINGS

A PERFECT NIGHT

Entering the bottom of the ninth inning on May 18, 2004, no Atlanta Braves batter had managed to get on base against Arizona pitcher Randy Johnson. That meant he was on the verge of a perfect game. Only 16 pitchers had thrown a perfect game since 1900. After Johnson retired the first two Atlanta batters, catcher Eddie Pérez strode to the plate. Johnson's first pitch was a strike. Next came a ball. Pérez fouled off Johnson's third offering. The fourth pitch was ball two. Then Johnson uncorked a 98-miles-per-hour fastball. Pérez had no chance. He swung and missed. Johnson had done it! His teammates mobbed him. "Not bad for being 40 years old," Johnson said. He is the oldest man to pitch a perfect game. (Since then, there have been another seven perfect games). He was named to the Baseball Hall of Fame in 2015.

RANDY JOHNSON
PITCHER
DIAMONDBACKS SEASONS: 1999–2004, 2007–08
HEIGHT: 6-FOOT-10
WEIGHT: 225 POUNDS
KEY STATS: 118–62 WIN-LOSS RECORD, 2.83 ERA, 2162 STRIKEOUTS, 4X CY YOUNG AWARD WINNER

EXTRA INNINGS

PAUL GOLDSCHMIDT
FIRST BASEMAN
DIAMONDBACKS SEASONS: 2011–18
HEIGHT: 6-FOOT-3
WEIGHT: 225 POUNDS
KEY STATS: .297 BATTING AVERAGE, 209 HOME RUNS, 710 RBIS, LED LEAGUE IN HOME RUNS (36) AND RBIS (110) IN 2013

HIDDEN GEM

Arizona didn't draft Paul Goldschmidt until the eighth round of the 2009 MLB Draft. But he rose rapidly in Arizona's farm system. He was called up to the majors late in 2011. His first at bat was a single. He homered the next day. Then he became just the third rookie to hit a grand slam in postseason play. Goldschmidt played like a first-rounder for the next seven seasons. He was a six-time All-Star. He received three Gold Glove Awards. Four times, he won the Silver Slugger award, given to the best offensive player at each position. His Goldy's Fund 4 Kids raises money for Phoenix Children's Hospital.

WORST TO FIRST

The Diamondbacks signed slugging third baseman Troy Glaus before the 2005 season. He hit 37 home runs. Glaus and infielder Tony Clark helped Arizona make a 26-game improvement. It finished 77–85. That was a move in the right direction, but the team remained out of the playoffs. The following year, Webb proved to be the bright spot in an otherwise mediocre 76–86 season. He led the league with 16 victories and won the Cy Young Award.

Arizona celebrated redesigned uniforms and Johnson's return in 2007. But he struggled with back injuries. Eventually, he underwent season-ending surgery. Webb took up some of the slack with 18 wins and a 3.01 ERA. The Diamondbacks also received inspired play from second baseman Orlando Hudson. He racked up 152 hits and earned a Gold Glove. Center fielder Chris Young hit 32 home runs and stole 27 bases in his first full MLB season.

The plucky young team managed to win 90 games that season. Arizona swept the Chicago Cubs in the NLDS. Then they faced the red-hot Colorado Rockies in the NLCS. Colorado swept the series in four games. But the Diamondbacks knew they had exceeded expectations by getting as far as they did. "It's something to write about," manager Bob Melvin told reporters after the NLCS. "There were two teams left in the National League, and we were one of them."

Arizona started 2008 with a 20–8 record. Webb won his first nine outings. He completed the season with a league-leading 22 wins. Fellow pitcher Dan Haren earned a career-high 16 wins in his first Diamondbacks season. Johnson

Third baseman Mark Reynolds

recovered and won 11 games. But the team could not maintain its initial success. Arizona ended 82–80. It barely missed the playoffs.

The Diamondbacks entered the 2009 season with high hopes. But Webb pitched just four innings on Opening Day. He left the game with a serious shoulder injury. It was his last MLB game. Outfielder Justin Upton hit 26 home runs and had 86 RBIs. Third baseman Mark Reynolds emerged as a powerhouse slugger, clubbing 44 home runs. Despite these efforts, the D-backs tumbled to the bottom of the division with a 70–92 mark.

Arizona was even worse in 2010. The team limped to 65 wins. The Diamondbacks set an unfortunate MLB record: players struck out 1,529 times during the season.

The Diamondbacks staged a remarkable turnaround in 2011. They went from worst to first in the division with a 94–68 record. Pitcher Ian Kennedy compiled a 21–4 record. Upton hit 31 homers. He finished fourth in Most Valuable Player (MVP) voting. But in the NLDS, Arizona fell to the Milwaukee Brewers in five games.

Pitcher Brandon Webb

EXTRA INNINGS

KETEL MARTE
SECOND BASE/SHORTSTOP
DIAMONDBACK SEASONS: 2017–PRESENT
HEIGHT: 6-FOOT-1
WEIGHT: 208 POUNDS
KEY STATS: .283 BATTING AVERAGE, 140 HOME RUNS, 515 RBIS, 2X ALL-STAR

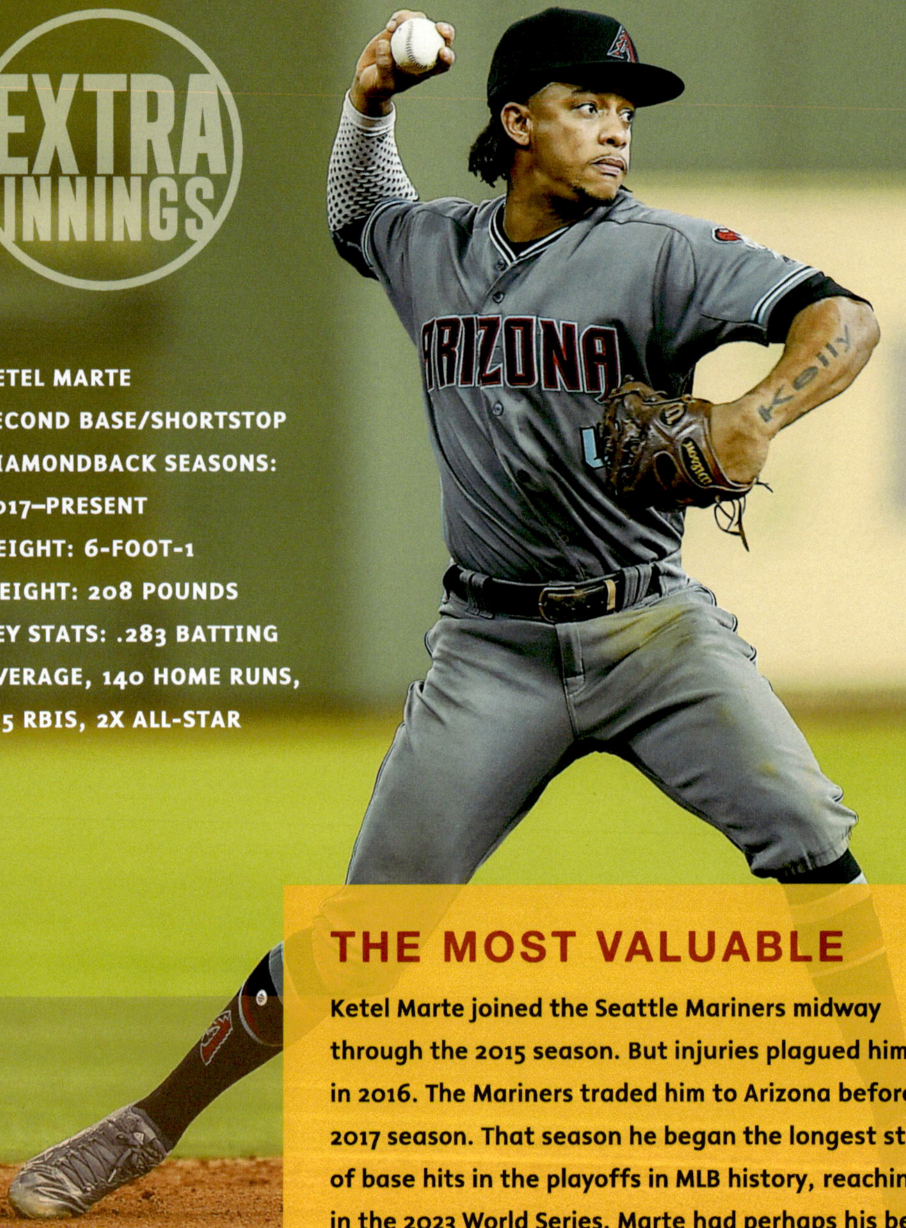

THE MOST VALUABLE

Ketel Marte joined the Seattle Mariners midway through the 2015 season. But injuries plagued him in 2016. The Mariners traded him to Arizona before the 2017 season. That season he began the longest streak of base hits in the playoffs in MLB history, reaching 20 in the 2023 World Series. Marte had perhaps his best season in 2024, with 36 home runs and 95 RBIs. He was named to the All-MLB First Team. Arizona barely missed the playoffs despite winning 89 games. "You talk about MVP—Most Valuable Player," said Arizona relief pitcher Ryan Thompson. "If you take Ketel off our team throughout the whole year, where would we be?"

RESHAPING THE ROSTER

Fans expected the team to bounce back in 2012. Two players in their first full seasons in Arizona did their part. One was first baseman Paul Goldschmidt. He batted .286 and smashed 20 homers. The other was infielder Aaron Hill. He hit .302 with 26 home runs. Hill became the first player since Babe Herman of the Brooklyn Robins (now the Los Angeles Dodgers) in 1931 to hit for the cycle (a single, double, triple, and home run in one game) twice in the same season. But the team was consistently inconsistent. It finished 81–81.

Once again, Arizona reshaped its roster. General manager Kevin Towers said that he was looking for "those type of players who understood the game and the scoreboard and what you need to do to help your club win that particular night." But once again, injuries haunted the team. Arizona repeated its 81–81 record in 2013. Goldschmidt emerged as a top-level player. He hit .302, slammed 36 homers, and drove in 125 runs. He was runner-up in MVP voting.

The Diamondbacks started 2014 at 5–18. They went downhill from there, finishing 64–98. It was their second-worst record. Arizona improved to 79–83 the following season. Team officials decided that they needed a stronger pitching rotation. They signed Zack Greinke to a six-year, $206.5 million deal. Its annual average of $34.4 million was the largest deal in MLB history at that time. Greinke won a relatively modest 13 games in 2016. Other newcomers also struggled. The team went just 69–93. Many people

Second baseman Orlando Hudson

Pitcher Zack Greinke

called it the most disappointing season in team history because of the high expectations they had before it began.

New general manager Mike Hazen made a couple of important trades. One was with the Seattle Mariners to get shortstop Ketel Marte. But the nucleus of the team stayed intact for the 2017 season. "The reason we kept the team together in the off-season was because we wanted to give these guys a chance to redeem what happened last season," Hazen said. "It came together pretty quickly." So quickly, in fact, that the team flipped its record from the previous year to 93–69. The Diamondbacks finished second in the NL West. They made their first playoff appearance in six years. Backed by four triples—the most in a playoff game since 1903—Arizona won the NL Wild Card game against Colorado. The Diamondbacks advanced to the NLDS. But the Dodgers swept them. "The bottom line is they were just a better team," said pitcher Archie Bradley. "It's a tough one to swallow."

Catcher Miguel Montero

D-backs

EXTRA INNINGS

LAW OF AVERAGES

In 2019, Arizona was called the "most average team" in baseball history. That's because they had a streak of 60 straight games where they were within two games above or below .500. That broke the previous MLB record of 56. The streak began on June 18 with a loss to the Colorado Rockies that made Arizona's record 38–36. On August 30, they defeated the Dodgers to rise to 69–66. In between, they were even at 30–30. "I guess that does mean that we are pretty steady," Diamondbacks manager Torey Lovullo said, "But I don't think I necessarily consider that a compliment." The D-backs went 16–11 the rest of the way to finish at 85–77.

BACK TO THE WORLD SERIES

Arizona fans had high hopes for 2018. The D-backs became the first NL team since the 1907 Cubs to win their first nine series. They led the division for most of the season. But September was brutal. The team won just 8 of 27 games. Arizona finished 82–80. It missed the playoffs.

The next season ended in a similar fashion. The team had an 85–77 record but missed the playoffs again.

The momentum of three straight winning seasons went away in 2020 with the COVID-19 pandemic. Arizona fell to 25–35 in the shortened season and finished far from playoff contention. The bottom fell out in 2021. The Diamondbacks went just 52–110. It was their worst record since 2004. It included an MLB-record away-game losing streak of 24 games.

It was almost a different story in 2022. Near the halfway point, the D-backs led the NL West with a 41–25 mark. They faded badly to finish 74–88.

In an especially tight race in 2023, Arizona lost their final four games. Yet they squeezed into the playoffs for the first time in 16 years. They were the third Wild Card team with an 84–78 mark. Three teams were just a game or two behind them. But once in the playoffs, Arizona ran wild. They swept both the Milwaukee Brewers and 100-win Dodgers. They defeated the Phillies in seven games to advance to the World Series for the first time since 2001. But they couldn't maintain the magic against the Texas Rangers. The teams split the first two games in Texas. With the next three at home, D-backs fans were optimistic. But the Rangers won all three to take the title. Yet just being in the

NLCS, GAME 7
ARIZONA DIAMONDBACKS
AT PHILADELPHIA PHILLIES
OCTOBER 24, 2023

EXTRA INNINGS

THE LONG WAIT IS OVER

The Diamondbacks took a quick 1–0 lead. Rookie of the Year outfielder Corbin Carroll scored on a force out in the first inning. The Phillies evened the score in the second, then took a 2–1 lead two innings later. Arizona knotted the score in the top of the fifth as Carroll singled home third baseman Emmanuel Rivera. Then the Diamondbacks took the lead as catcher Gabriel Moreno's single plated Carroll. Two innings later, Carroll's sacrifice fly scored shortstop Geraldo Perdomo for a 4–2 lead. Kevin Ginkel pitched two innings of shutout relief and Paul Seward closed out the game with a perfect ninth to send the Diamondbacks back to the World Series for the first time in 22 years. "We did it!" said Carroll. "Just believe in each other, believe in our guys."

Second baseman **Ketel Marte**

World Series was a remarkable achievement for a team that had won only 52 games two years prior.

At one point in 2024, Arizona had a seven-game lead in the Wild Card race. They faded to 89–73 and a three-way tie with the Braves and Mets for the two remaining spots. But both teams had the tiebreaker edge over the D-backs. Still, first baseman Christian Walker won his third Gold Glove. His 26 homers marked the third straight season with at least 25 long balls. Third baseman Eugenio Suárez hit 30 home runs and drove in 100 runs after joining the Diamondbacks.

Throughout their short history in the desert, the Diamondbacks have had several hot seasons. Arizona fans have been willing to stick with their team during its cold spells as well. They feel confident that the Diamondbacks will soon snake their way back to the top.

Third baseman Eugenio Suárez

INDEX

All-Stars, 10, 16, 20
"Baby Backs", 14
Bell, Jay, 11, 13
Benes, Andy, 13
Bradley, Archie, 24
Clark, Tony, 17
Colangelo, Jerry, 11, 13
COVID-19, 28
Cy Young Award, 13, 15, 17
division championships, 13, 14, 18, 28
Finley, Steve, 13
Garagiola, Joe Jr., 14
Glaus, Troy, 17
Gold Glove award, 13, 16, 17, 31
Goldschmidt, Paul, 16, 21
Gonzalez, Luis, 8, 9, 10, 11, 13, 14
Greinke, Zack, 21, 24
Haren, Dan, 17
Hazen, Mike, 24
Hill, Aaron, 21
Hudson, Orlando, 17, 23
Johnson, Randy, 13, 14, 15, 17
    perfect game, 14, 15
Kennedy, Ian, 18
Melvin, Bob, 17
MLB Draft, 16
playoffs, 13, 14, 17, 18, 20, 24, 28
    National League Championship Series (NLCS), 14
    National League Division Series (NLDS), 13
    Wild Card, 24, 28, 31
retired numbers, 10
Reynolds, Mark, 18
Schilling, Curt, 11, 13, 14
Silver Slugger award, 16
team name, 8, 11
Towers, Kevin, 21
Upton, Justin, 18
Webb, Brandon, 14, 17, 18
Williams, Matt, 13
Womack, Tony, 8, 13
World Series, 8, 11, 13, 14, 20, 28, 29